A Good Season

poems by

Gail Gehlken

Finishing Line Press
Georgetown, Kentucky

A Good Season

Copyright © 2016 by Gail Gehlken
ISBN 978-1-944251-19-2 First Edition
All rights reserved under International and Pan-American Copyright Conventions.
No part of this book may be reproduced in any manner whatsoever without written permission from the publisher, except in the case of brief quotations embodied in critical articles and reviews.

Editor: Christen Kincaid

Cover Art: Amy Gehlken

Author Photo: Jack L. Gehlken

Cover Design: Elizabeth Maines

Printed in the USA on acid-free paper.
Order online: www.finishinglinepress.com
         also available on amazon.com

                Author inquiries and mail orders:
                      Finishing Line Press
                          P. O. Box 1626
                Georgetown, Kentucky 40324
                            U. S. A.

Table of Contents

In January 1
Wool Blanket Brown...2
Double Exposure 3
The Cold Is Back 4
From the Wood-burning Stove..5
Spring Can Wait..6

Well, Glory Be! 7
Purple Tops of White Globes..8
First in Line...9
When Gardenias Bloom..10
Eye to Eye 11
A Green Feast...12
Chinaberry Blues..14
Ending the Drought 15
We Know Our Places 16
Walter Anderson's Cat 17
Forcing Priorities..18
Washington Avenue 19
What's the Difference Anyway?...20

As September Passes 21
A Cat's November Meditation 22
From Mississippi Sound..23
Leggy and Leafless...24
A Good Season 25
Black Silks...26
She Always Wears Brown..27
Fall Plantings..28
The Long Harvest..29

For Jack, Amy, Seth, and Neil

In January

Along the Alabama Gulf Coast
while icy rains fall
and moaning winds
push low fronts through
making way for even colder air,
robins come in flocks.

With their rounding russet breasts
thrust in pride,
they begin to settle
covering the ground
like a feathered blanket,
yet continue to lift a bit in sections
moving only inches
as if adjusting corners of a picnic quilt.

Then settling again,
they eat.

Wool Blanket Brown

Fresh air molds
into the chambers of my lungs
as once green crinums, buckeye trees,
and jasmines camouflage themselves
in ochre and wool blanket brown.

With no care for the cold,
I take my shovel
into this perfect part of winter,
the days between New Year's
and Valentine's,
when the garden's sap
sinks deepest
and caps the veins,
not to be harmed

as I dig at will
moving daylilies,
adding green-throated reds
next to lemon yellows,
plant rooted Maggie rose cuttings
beside Belinda's Dream
and divide crowded ginger lily tubers
rising out of the ground.

Working behind spring's door
in the safety of the cold,
I carry out my plan.
Then I wait for early signs of green.

Double Exposure

Black satin birds
with wings blushing green
flew between me and the sun.
A full dozen circled
over emerald, pine-needled
tree top seas
as their silhouettes swam
        in the branches below.

I watched their stenciled shapes
against the five o'clock sky
until the black satin birds
with blushing, green wings
settled in the upper tiers
of long-leaf pines
        reclaiming their shadows

The Cold Is Back

This morning I walked out
to the front garden
to see what frost had done.

No surprises for me
since I had read wintry signs
          from my window
telling me tender angel trumpets
wear limp army-green leaves
with drooping weeping creamy blooms.

Yet, I welcome this forced cleansing
          by November's cold
as I begin to clear away stubbles
of summer's pink cleome and red zinnias
without the guilt of taking the life
of faded lingering blooms.

From the Wood-burning Stove

heated fingers
reach up and out
pushing cooler air
to the wall and out the door
into the empty hall
moving like smoke
curling around worn leather-bound books
and brass lady bells
clustered together
as if for warmth.

Spring can wait

a little longer this year
while I praise God
for narcissus breaking out
of onion-skinned bulbed cocoons
where they secretly stored
their purest whites
and pastel yellows.

Well, Glory Be!

To weeds, ever patient to stay
but yielding when pulled

To dirt, rich in microbes,
tangled with earthworms

To seeds, coded for pumpkins, butterbeans,
cucumbers and butternut squash

To lavender blooms on leafy green stems
hiding new red potatoes maturing underground

To the feathers of speckled Sussex,
Wellsummer, and mottled Java hens

To Satsuma trees and Stuart pecans,
cardinals, mockingbirds, and Carolina wrens.

I'm amazed.
Well, glory be!

Purple Tops of White Globes

Yesterday I planted seeds,
dark and small as coffee grounds,
letting them roll into my hand
from a paper packet
picturing purple-top
white-globe turnips,
roots and leaves.

Sprinkling the rolling specks
in a shallow trench,
I covered them with leafy mulch,
gave the row a light tap
with my foot
and a spray of water.

Then walked away to wait.

First in Line

Blooming before the red buds
and white Bradford pears,
Japanese magnolias
seize color-starved eyes,
grown tired of fossil grays

and send their lavender lights
through the chill and drizzle
of February's fog
with blooms in purples and pinks
lifted high on leafless limb tips
like candelabra arms.

In defying winter's attempts to stay,
tulip trees throw their palm-sized petals
to the cold ground
sealing the end to winter's bleakness,
with the promise of spring.

When Gardenias Bloom

their scent hangs heavy
in May's warming humid air
where flowers cluster in bunches
like muscadines
ripening on the vine.

When gardenias bloom,
I break off limbs
weighted with white velvety petals
and shake off bumble bees
worshipping
at yellow temple-shaped stamens.

When gardenias bloom,
I remember Grandmother's
unpainted, clap-board house
with its gray, streaked, wooden fence
cut to a picket point.

As gardenias bloom,
I become a child in a porch swing
where now I can touch my toes to the floor
as the chains see-saw
on the rusting ceiling hooks.

When gardenias bloom,
their sweetness makes me bold,
and I drink the scented air
that reminds me
where I have been.

Eye to Eye

While taking photographs
I watched a monarch and a swallowtail
that seemed to be debating
over which zinnia tasted sweeter,
the pink one or the yellow.

I could tell that neither creature
could quite agree,
flitting from bloom to bloom
sampling the orange
and then the red,

before settling the score
by dipping into pink Fairy roses
and white buddleia
infused with such sweetness,
they decided to share.

A Green Feast

"Do you walk to pass the time?"
someone asked and
I answered,
"No, I walk to save my life."

I walk through my garden
where Monday last
I planted willow butterbeans,
zucchini and patty pan squash

and on Tuesday
I drove stakes to support Goliath tomatoes,
jalapeno peppers, and Black Beauty eggplants
before they flopped.

In walking I pause to marvel
at the work of the pitchfork
and the rich rows of sod and manure
opened on Wednesday for planting

G90 sweet corn and Clemson spineless okra.
On Thursday, I picked the last of the sugar snaps
from drought-ridden,
yellowing vines still clinging

to wire fencing.
Walking into Friday
I cleared away
turnips and radishes gone to seed,
not good for cooking but perfect
as a green feast for Partridge Rock hens
in exchange for their smooth brown eggs.

Then beside the guinea's house, I stopped to add
sage, thyme, and basil plants
creating a delicious fragrant place
for a Saturday pause.

On Sunday
I walk to celebrate
a week of walking,
rejoicing that I have no empty hours
just to pass time.

Chinaberry Blues

Pull up a chair
in the South
in summer.
Feel the cool breeze.
Watch small blue-eyed flowers
wink from umbrella-shaped trees
where leaves overlap leaves
like thatch over thatch
sheltering wind swept ground.

Heat bearing down on tanned skin,
black-eyed peas need picking
but just stay awhile in the shade,
wink back at lavender-blue clusters
hanging overhead.
In the South
in summer,
nothing's like Chinaberry blues.

Watermelons swell
from drinking June's rain
while seeds harden,
pulp pinks,
and the rinds' underbellies turn yellow.
But sweet juicy melons
leave me longing for the shade
in the South
in summer
under Chinaberry trees.
Nothing's like Chinaberry blues.

Ending the drought

I sit waiting
watching west winds sweep
shriveled leaves about
before funneling them into piles.
Rain's coming.

Small drops dot the porch.
Then the plop plop
of larger drops bend
the leaves of bleeding hearts
whose red clay pots drink
like thirsty up-turned mouths.

On the steps a bucket
makes its own water music
with plink plink
rescuing the tin cup
from its rusting circle at the bottom
as it twirls
coming higher and higher.

The pitch of the storm's rumbling thunder
and sizzling lightning
drives me into the house
but the melody in the rain
makes dark clouds welcome
after dusty days.

We Know Our Places

Amadeus and I
don't talk much,
yet we know our places.
He lies wherever he pleases
stretching his spotted black and white body
like a row of piano keys
and squints through a tiny slit
of one green eye
      as I pass by

while I change beds, wash clothes,
sweep floors, cook, and do dishes
working all around him
yet he never moves
except to peek at me,
winking one green eye as I pass by.
And I?
Well, I just step right over him
wherever he decides to lie.
      We do know our places.

Walter Anderson's Cat

Robinson traipses away,
his tail's tip in a fish hook curl.
Then looking back
through a slit of his green eye,
       he smiles.

Forcing Priorities

    Eating cantaloupe in the dark
          out of a coffee cup,
I pierce creamy chunks
with deliberate precision
concentrating only
on the cool, smooth taste,
not its peachy, orange flesh
or the tan, ribboned-ridged hull
       that held it.

Washington Avenue
Walter Anderson Museum
Ocean Springs, MS

I didn't go in the museum today,
just stood outside,
letting images from earlier visits
converge in my mind
of the secret room's murals

with deer, raccoons, blueberries,
every space an eye, a petal,
a butterfly's wing,
blackberries,
Blue Jays,
green toads,
red zinnia on the ceiling,
bicycle,
row boat,

all stored, recalled, and
painted in privacy
like a silent prayer.

What's the Difference Anyway?

What difference does it make?
I ask myself at times
if butterflies come to taste
orange zinnia blooms
on lazy July afternoons.

Does it make a difference
if green satin-backed
hummingbirds drink
from Red Crimson honeysuckle trumpets
trimmed with yellow edges,
        or not?

Or if I bring cut flowers
into the kitchen
and find a bumble bee
dazed in intoxication
of purple garden phlox's perfume
or not ?

Oh! What a difference!

As September Passes

Pumpkins swell like helium balloons
   growing inches overnight
   after sneaking huge puffs
   of humid late summer air.
When no one's looking
   hunter green ridges begin to rise
   under the cover of a layered silver-striped leaf canopy
   hiding subtle caramel-colored streaks
   like a sunburst's glow at the bloom end,
      the birth scar.

A Cat's November Morning Meditation

I need time to sit
on my windowsill
like Tig does,
winking at sun streamers
falling through leafless limbs
blinking the brightness into dimmer light.
As he turns his tabby head
to block the steady breeze,
he postures against the chill,

yet he returns morning after morning
never wavering one brick left or right
and like sunrise,
he reminds me to meditate.

From Mississippi Sound

I live under pecan trees
whose leaves flutter
with the slightest breeze
from sea winds drifting
north from Mississippi Sound.

But every morning
as a commuter
I leave before daybreak
take my place in line
on the interstate
and look at red tail lights ahead
while someone behind
looks at mine.

As my car follows another
into the concrete city
of motors and graffiti
I think of returning
to the shelter of my trees
and soft bayou breezes,
sanctuary.

Leggy and Leafless

I hesitate to cut the old shrub rose,
       looking leggy and leafless,
preferring instead to wait
for the rose hips

to swell and turn red
       as the season closes,
shutting down,
gathering energy
to come again

much like the thick seed pods
       on August lilies
grow heavy and droop down
before they dry and crack open,
releasing seed to the ground
to sleep the winter
waiting for spring
to feed and grow again.

A Good Season

The fig tree drops its leaves
but doesn't seem to care
as an October south wind
whips them loose
leaving open spaces,
exposing dark limbs
curling out and up
reaching like hands
in praise of the past season

when brown turkey figs
ripened full and round
showing stretch marks
where swelling skins bulged
and held back syrupy juices
as yellow jackets congregated
on overripe figs in high places
my fingers could not reach,
in places I left
as the mockingbirds' share,
where they nested and sang
their hymns for the good season.

Black Silks

While driving
on a four-lane highway,
I saw a flock of black starlings
rising and sinking
      on air currents,
falling in drifts
like Updike's "Great Scarf of Birds."

While watching them move,
flowing like silk steamers,
I felt a surge of delight
      in knowing a poet
captured the image
by sculpting in words.

She Always Wears Brown

While drinking my morning coffee
I hear the same clear
"Jimmee, jimmee, jimmee,"
from the Caroline wren
who never varies lyrics

and always wears brown
blending with pecan tree bark,
rose stems, and plum branches
as she darts about the garden,
busy with rituals as if in dance.

Coming near my window,
she pokes around in planters
of silvery lamb's ear,
red geraniums, and wax begonias
looking for gypsy moths hiding there.

"Jimmee, jimmee, jimmee"
she calls again and again
with clarity, confidence
and pride in her talents,
delighting in being herself.

"Jimmee, jimmee, jimmee"
a matching call comes across the garden.
She tilts her head to one side,
fluffs her feathers. Returning his
"Jimmee, jimmee, jimmee,"
she waits.

Fall Plantings

Morris heading cabbage
Georgia collards
Curly leaf mustard
Romaine lettuce
Multiplying onions,
    from saved seed,
Egyptian walking onions
Swiss chard
Spinach
Kale,
    curly leaf and straight,
Danvers carrots
Easter egg radishes
Apollo broccoli
Rutabagas
Purple top white-globe turnips
Rosemary
Nasturtium leaves
    breaking the ground.

Without a winter garden
I would starve
for the color and taste of green.

The Long Harvest

On the first day of November
I chop red and green cayenne
while a pot of white vinegar simmers
sending stringent fumes
piercing through the house
like paint thinner.

Even with gloved hands
my fingers tingle
from the heat of opened veins
and bruised seeds
as I push peppers into cruets
and slender-necked bottles
before funneling the vinegar
over the chilies to steep

like water poured
over Earl Grey
in the Desert Rose teacup
I placed beside my chair
where I'll rest
from the long harvest.

Gail **Gehlken's** poetry appeared in the *Birmingham Arts Journal, Literary Mobile, Whoever Remembers Us: Anthology of Alabama Poets, Alabama Sampler,* and *Potpourri Literary Journal.*

Finishing Line Press published her chapbook, *Standing Stones,* in 2011.

www.ingramcontent.com/pod-product-compliance
Lightning Source LLC
Chambersburg PA
CBHW060225050426
42446CB00013B/3174